A DE-TAILED ACCOU
OF
MANX CATS

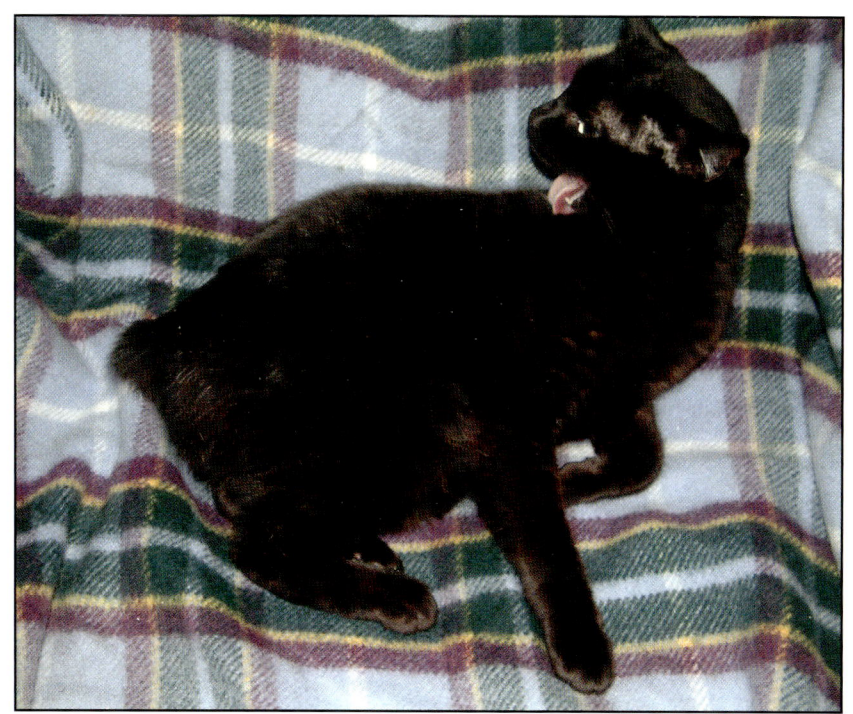

SARA GOODWINS

Loaghtan Books
Caardee, Dreemskerry Hill
Maughold
Isle of Man
IM7 1BE
Published by Loaghtan Books

First published: March 2013
Reprinted: May 2017
Reprinted: April 2024

Copyright © Sara Goodwins 2013

All rights reserved. No part of this publication may be reproduced, stored on a retrieval system or transmitted in any form or by any means without prior permission of the publishers.

Typesetting and origination by:
Loaghtan Books

Printed and bound by:
Short Run Press
Website: www.loaghtanbooks.com

ISBN: 978 1 908060 42 6

In memory of
Peter Tucker
who loved Manx cats

Front cover and pages 9, 10 and 17: Manx cat Troubs, originally an unwanted cat called 'Trouble', but rescued and lived out her life happily in Ramsey. *Photograph © P.B. Tucker*

Rear cover: Shorthair (left) and longhair Manx kittens; longhair Manx are sometimes called Cymric. Owned by Kay DeVilbiss, Minus DeTails, Texas. *Photograph © Helmi Flick Cat Photography*

Title page: Scadoo – 'Shadow' in Manx – lying on a Manx tartan blanket. *Photograph © P.B. Tucker*

CONTENTS

	Acknowledgements	4
I	The History	5
II	The Manx Cat today	13
III	Folklore	22
	Selected Bibliography	32

Hoofprint series
A De-tailed Account of Manx Cats
Things to do with Vikings
Three Legs Good; the story of the Manx triskelion
Mann with Altitude
Two Fish for the Summit; life and work on the Manx mountain
A Manx A-B-C-Dery; an Alphabetical Tour of the Isle of Man
Cross Purposes; an introduction to mediaeval Manx crosses
A Key to Tynwald

ACKNOWLEDGEMENTS

With thanks to Moira and David Ashworth and Irene Spiers for the idea for the book, and for being so helpful with all aspects of the children's competition, to Mary Cousins for being such an excellent judge despite it being an extremely busy time for her, and to Jo Overty for her help and advice with the children's story competition; it would have been very much more difficult to arrange without her.

Many thanks also to Peter Tucker for showering us with photographs which we could use for illustrations. Thank you to Helmi Flick, professional cat photographer, not only for allowing us to reproduce some of her superb work free of charge, but also for coming up trumps with the photograph of the Japanese Bobtail when we'd almost given up hope of finding one. Thank you to Tracy and Colin Wood for making a similar search for a picture of a Norwegian Forest Cat so quick and simple.

Thank you to Frances Chambers for allowing us to publish her gem of a poem *Transmogrification*, and to Robert Kelly for permission to reproduce three poems from his book *Tails of the Tailless*.

Finally, thank you to all the children in years 5 and 6 at school in the Isle of Man who wrote stories for the Manx cat story competition, and to their schools, parents or guardians who helped them to enter. We had many excellent entries and are only sorry that you couldn't all win.

PART I

THE HISTORY

Cats are not native to the Isle of Man. That sounds obvious, but the fact is important to understanding why the island developed its own breed. Cats have been living with human beings for roughly ten thousand years. They were first domesticated, or more probably decided that human beings were a helpful species to work with, in the Middle East in the area known to historians as the Fertile Crescent. The region is an arc curving to include the Euphrates and the Nile and includes parts of Kuwait, Iraq, Iran, Syria, Jordan, Israel, Lebanon and Egypt. The area is sometimes called the Cradle of Civilisation, as most people are thought to have spread from the Fertile Crescent too.

About ten thousand years ago human beings changed from hunter/gatherers to farmers. As farmers they stored far more food than had previously been the case, food which was attractive to vermin. Following the laws of the food chain, vermin attracted cats. The two higher species tolerated each other; humans because cats hunted the mice and rats which ate the stored food, cats because human settlements gave them access to a plentiful and reliable source of prey. When people began to spread out of Africa, the cats followed them.

Manx moggies

No-one knows when cats were first introduced to the Isle of Man, but the Vikings probably played a large part in increasing the island's feline population. Invaders from Norway first arrived on Mann in 798 and from raiding turned to invading, quickly establishing settlements all over the island. The Vikings liked cats. According to one of the Norse legends, Freyja, the goddess of love, rode in a chariot pulled by two wildcats. Kittens were often considered a good gift for a new bride; a new home would mean a new need for reliable pest control. Vikings were also fashion conscious and there is some evidence at Whithorn in Wigton, the part of Scotland just north of the Isle of Man, that some cats were bred by Norsemen for their pelts. Certainly in medieval times cat fur was popular as a trimming on clothing. The popularity of cats with Mann's new Viking inhabitants probably means that cats have lived on the island for at least twelve hundred years and possibly a good deal longer.

The breed probably most familiar to Vikings was the *Norsk Skogkatt* (sometimes spelt *skaukatt*) or Norwegian Forest cats. They are large, heavy cats, tailed, with a long-haired extremely waterproof double coat to help cope with outdoor conditions in a cold, wet climate. What makes them particularly interesting from a Manx cat point of view, is that the Norwegian Forest cat's hind legs are longer than its forelegs. So are those of a Manx. Both breeds also have double coats, share a liking for water, tend not to vocalise loudly and have certain dog-like characteristics such as following their human companions

Norwegian Forest Cat, Norsvana Sugar Sparkle. Photograph © Tracy and Colin Wood. Norsvana Norwegian Forest Cats, North Yorkshire

around. All of these traits could be coincidences, but it is at least possible that the *Norsk Skogkatt* makes up part of the ancestry of the Manx.

The first references to Manx cats being tailless seem to have occurred in the early eighteenth century, although cats without tails may of course have been around for some time in small but growing numbers. 'Cat' in Manx is *kayt* and all cats on the island appeared to have been referred to as such until around 1730-1750, when a new word, *stubbin*, crept into Manx from the English 'stubby'. In Manx *stubbin* is a cat with no tail or only a short stump. No-one invents a word for something which doesn't exist, so it seems likely that tailless cats became common enough in the first half of the eighteenth century for people to need a word to distinguish them from their tailed cousins.

The cat's earliest recorded appearance in England – it may have arrived earlier and not been noted – is thanks to J.M.W. Turner. The painter owned three houses in London, two in Harley Street and one in Queen Anne Street, the gardens of which backed onto each other. Turner used the gardens to move between his houses without going out onto the street and to avoid the corner house which was owned by someone else. In the chapter in Lewis Hind's *Turner's Golden Visions*, which concerns events of 1810, Hind says: 'Two ladies, Mrs R– and Mrs H– once paid [Turner] a visit in Harley Street… and were shown into a large sitting room without a fire. This was in the depths of winter; and lying about in various places were several cats without tails… One of the ladies bestowing some notice upon the cats, [Turner] was induced to remark that he had seven, and that they came from the Isle of Man.'

The shortening of the tail in Manx cats appears to have arisen spontaneously and to be the result of what is known in genetics as the founder effect, where distinctive differences arise from a limited gene pool. If there is little variation in the gene pool then the differences can become fixed. As the gene pool of cats on the Isle of Man was relatively small, short tails or none became much more common as the result of inbreeding. The fact that Mann is an island prevented its cat population from breeding much with its cousins from over the water who had not developed the short-tailed gene.

In the early eighteenth century, when the gene shift had newly occurred, Manx cats probably had a short stump of a tail; normal patterns of genetic mutation, plus the use of the word *stubbin* seems to indicate this. True taillessness may therefore have been the result of deliberate breeding; tailless cats were a novelty and everyone wanted one.

Widely travelled

There has been speculation that the Manx breed is related to or descended from the bobtail cats common throughout Asia. Such cats, most notably the Japanese Bobtail, show thin twisted tails. In the Bobtail a tail of normal or near normal length is twisted or coiled to form a shape like a rabbit's scut. Sometimes the tail can be uncurled by hand, but this is usually painful, or at best uncomfortable for the animal, and often impossible to do; the tail will resume its curled shape when not handled. Although the Asian bobtail varieties have been around a lot longer than the Manx cat – the Japanese Bobtail, for example, is thought to have existed for a thousand years and appears in antique pictures and illustrations – they are unlikely to be the ancestors of the Manx because of the genetic make up of the two breeds. The different tail shapes of the bobtail breeds and the Manx are the result of difference genetic mutations. The gene which caused the tail mutation in the Asian breeds is recessive; in the Manx the gene is dominant (see page 18). Put simply, the two breeds cannot be related.

Early in the nineteenth century there were also reports of cats in Cornwall which lacked tails. This is possibly an independent genetic mutation, but seems more likely to be the result of trade between the two Celtic areas. Metalworking was known to occur on the Isle of Man during the Bronze Age and later. Bronze is made from copper and tin, with lead added to make the alloy easier to pour. Mann has its own copper and lead, but the only two sources of tin in Europe are south-west Britain, particularly Cornwall, and Spain. By sea, Kernow (the Cornish for Cornwall) is almost in a straight line from Mannin (the Manx for Mann) and the winds and currents make such a passage easy. The easy seaway was probably why the Celts landed in south west England in the first place. And it was a two-way exchange.

Japanese Bobtail, Gulfcats Missy. Owned by Toni and Paul Huff, Gulfcats, South Texas. Photograph © Helmi Flick Cat Photography

Not only did the Manx trade with Cornwall, but Cornish miners often sought work in Manx mines. What with trading, mining, fishing and a related language, the two Celtic communities probably had a lot in common. Manx cats were considered very good mousers and it's quite possible that various animals were taken to Cornwall as pets, presents and curiosities, and left their genes there.

A significant community of tailless cats, thought to be descended from their Manx cousins, also exists on Reersø, in the Kalundborg region of Denmark. About fifty miles west of Copenhagen, Reersø, formerly a small island, is linked to neighbouring Zealand by a peninsula which floods in bad weather. The cats were supposed to have arrived on the island around 200 years ago – some think 120 years ago – after a farmer bought a pregnant queen from a sailor. Alternatively the cats may have come ashore after a Manx ship was wrecked in Storebælt (the Great Belt), another instance of shipwreck playing a possible part in Manx cat history (see page 25).

Another home of the Manx cat was and is North America. Emigration has always been a fact of life for the Manx but, in the early nineteenth century, the trickle of emigrants became a flood as poor harvests, rising prices and the lack of work elsewhere put many small farmers out of business. It has been suggested that the Manx emigrants took their special cats with them, and so were responsible for the animal crossing the Atlantic. It's a lovely idea, but doesn't seem very likely. A poor family, carrying all their worldly possessions, huddled in whatever corner of a ship their meagre wealth could pay for, would surely have only the resources to transport and feed family members, and not livestock or pets. Pet cats did exist, of course, but those whose cat was either a pampered favourite, or their sole source of companionship were rarely those driven to emigration.

It seems more reasonable to think that the Manx cats in North America are there because people liked them and deliberately imported the breed, rather than as the descendants of animals toted with difficulty by those emigrating out of poverty. Some accounts do in fact support a deliberate importation of Manx cats. In the early nineteenth century, in the Toms River area of New Jersey, the Hurley family had expanded beyond farming to owning their own small fleet of merchant ships. On one trip to Britain one of their ships took back several tailless cats, said to have come from the Isle of Man. The date was 1820

FELINE DIPLOMACY

When the Home Office first moved into its London premises in 1883, the building was infested with vermin and official permission was sought to get an office cat to deal with the problem. Permission duly granted, the first cat arrived. Peter was an ordinary black moggy and was given shelter and water, but expected largely to feed himself on mice, which was after all the reason for his 'employment'.

By 1929 the supply of fresh mice was found to be not quite limitless, and the Peter of the day was granted a food allowance. A letter from the Treasury says: 'I see no objection to your office keeper being allowed 1d a day from petty cash towards the maintenance of an efficient office cat.' A succession of feline incumbents of the post followed, all black, all male and all called Peter. Some became famous with the public but gifts were politely refused on the grounds that 'since Peter is an established civil servant he cannot be allowed to receive gifts'. Humorous accusations of bribery were met with the polite response 'there have been no annual reports on Peter's conduct... but there may be a security risk, inasmuch as though there is some evidence that he has been doctored, there is none whatever that he has been vetted'!

In 1964 the latest Peter died from a liver infection and the Lieutenant Governor of the Isle of Man, Sir Ronald Garvey, offered the Home Office a Manx cat as a replacement. The offer was accepted and *Manninagh KateDhu* took up residence. The name means 'Manx black cat', and the new employee was the correct colour for the job. However, during the 1960s the feminist movement had been growing and, for the first time, the Home Office cat was female. Unfortunately Peta – the Home Office insisted that her name should continue the tradition as far as possible – wasn't a howling, or should that be a meowing, success. Despite receiving a salary double that of her predecessors (five shillings instead of half a crown) she was accused of being noisy, lazy and not well house trained; the last possibly the fault of her taillessness (see page 18). However, being the gift of the Manx government Peta had 'diplomatic status' so she was retired and went to live with a Civil Service colleague.

She turned out to be the last official Home Office mouser as they moved to 50 Queen Anne's Gate in 1976. As the premises were brand new and purpose built, it was felt that they should be free of vermin so an official cat was not needed and almost a century of tradition ended.

and is the earliest known account of Manx cats in America. The cats flourished on the Hurley farm and, as Manx cats have a reputation of being excellent hunters, were regularly given as dowries whenever a member of the family married, a tradition which harks back to the Vikings (see page 5).

Their excellence as hunters was the main reason why Manx cats were often found on farms. They were working animals, tolerated to keep down rats and mice, often feral, and seldom or never handled. Before the days of routine neutering to prevent unwanted litters, colonies of feral cats were much more common.

Descendants of cats from the Douglas Horse Tram stables, for example, eventually formed their own colony in the 1950s and could often be seen hunting on the rocks at Port Jack and Onchan Head. Cats from the colony were seen routinely to tackle seagulls, as the longer back legs of Manx cats make them formidable jumpers; some have been even known to take prey such as bats and small birds on the wing.

Farms were not the only concerns which wanted a reliable cat to keep down mice; it was quite normal for businesses in towns to have their own 'in-house' feline employee to deal with vermin. Dumbell's Bank, Castle Rushen when it was the seat of government, the English House of Lords (in the 1940s) and the Home Office in Whitehall (in the 1960s) all kept an official office cat.

The Manx cats' hunting skills also made them valuable as ships' cats. On long voyages where all provisions had to be carried and where rats could make a real difference to how much sailors got to eat, cats had long been considered as valuable ship-board pest control. Many vessels considered a ship's cat

> **FROM THE *SYDNEY MORNING HERALD* OF FRIDAY 17 OCTOBER 1958**
>
> **'TALE OF MANX CAT WITH HAPPY ENDING**
>
> **MELBOURNE, Thursday. Four grinning seaman were waiting with open arms when a Manx cat ran down the gangway of a T.A.A. Viscount airliner which reached Melbourne tonight.**
>
> Their "mothering duties" were over for they had been looking after the cat's kittens for almost a week. The cat – "Professor" – was left behind on a Cairns' wharf when the freighter *Cronulla* sailed for Melbourne last week. She had given birth to the kittens shortly before.
>
> The crew immediately went into action. They took the kittens into their care and radioed to ships' agents in Cairns to have Professor flown to Melbourne – at their expense.
>
> As soon as the plane landed tonight the men took Professor to their ship...'

The History

as essential and treated them as respected members of the crew. Most sailors, too, looked on their furry shipmate as a playful and entertaining companion. Sailors are notoriously superstitious and a cat was also considered to bring a vessel good luck. Quite apart from their hunting ability, Manx cats were particularly popular ships' cats, as a common naval belief was that a cat could start a storm using magic stored in its tail. No tail, no storm-starting powers!

It wasn't only among merchant vessels that ships' cats were valued. Such animals had official standing with the Royal Navy and several Manx cats have served aboard Royal Naval vessels, a series of them, appropriately enough, on the minelayer *HMS Manxman*. Even the ship's cat on the royal yacht *Britannia* was a tabby Manx cat, presented to the Queen Mother when she visited Castletown in 1963. It was named, appropriately enough, *Schickrys*, which is Manx for 'sure' or 'certain'. Not only is it a good omen for a mouser, it's also the Castletown town motto. The ubiquity of ships' cats ended in 1975 when new quarantine laws were introduced by various countries, complicating the arrival of animals in port.

Cat fancy

The first recorded cat show took place at St Giles' Fair, Winchester, England in 1598, although we don't know what form it took, nor how the cats were judged; whether on appearance or hunting ability. It was nearly three hundred years later, in July 1871, that Harrison Weir organised the first cat show in Britain, where cats were judged against specified criteria. In 1887 he founded the National Cat Club, and two years later wrote *Our Cats and All About Them*. Illustrated with numerous line drawings, the book was the first to describe the different varieties of cats, including the Manx cat, and listed the various points which distinguished the breed. Of the Manx cat he states: 'I have examined a number of specimens sent for exhibition at the Crystal Palace and other cat shows, and found in some a very short, thin, twisted tail, in others a mere excrescence, and some with an appendage more like a knob'. Contrary to what might be the opinion today, Weir considered a Manx cat with a short stump of a tail as not a true Manx, while those with a 'short, thin, twisted tail that cannot be straightened' were acceptably part of the breed.

Although it may not have looked quite the same as it does today, the Manx cat was one of the few breeds to be regularly shown in Victorian cat shows in England. In the earliest shows there were usually six acceptable breeds: two longhaired; the Angora and the Persian, and four shorthaired; the Manx, the Siamese, the Archangel (as the Maltese or Russian Blue was called) and the

'domestic shorthair'. However the number of breeds and classes very soon proliferated. The first Manx to become a champion was a silver tabby kitten called Bonhaki who was owned by a keeper at London Zoo. The show was held in the Royal Botanical Gardens and the judge was Louis Wain, famous for his drawings of anthropomorphised cats (see page 12).

At the beginning of the twentieth century, cat shows in America also grew rapidly in popularity and also regularly featured the Manx as a named breed. On both sides of the pond, judges were warned to watch for unscrupulous owners who had docked a newly-born kitten's tail in an effort to present it as a Manx, regardless of the fact that the mere lack of a tail is not the only thing which distinguishes the breed.

During the nineteenth and twentieth centuries the Manx government actively used the Manx cat to promote the island. Cats were given as gifts to famous people – John Wayne, Walt Disney and Edward VIII, when he was Prince of Wales, all received one – and tourists were encouraged to take one home. So many tailless cats left the island that there was some concern that there would not be enough of a breeding population left, particularly if the dangers of the cat population being decimated by epidemic were taken into consideration. As a result, the Isle of Man government set up the Manx cattery to perpetuate the breed. The government already had an

BREED STANDARD IN THE NINETEENTH CENTURY

Breed standard for the Manx cat in the first cat shows in the 1880s. Compare it with the European standard for the breed today on page 13.

Feature	Characteristics	Points
Head	Small, round, but tapering towards the lips, rather broad across the eyes, nose medium length, ears rather small, broad at base and sloping upwards to a point	10
Eyes	According to colour, as shown in other varieties	10
Fur	Short, of even length, smooth, silky and glossy	10
Colour	To range the same as other short-haired cats, if self, same as self, if marked same as the marked varieties, with less points, allowing for the tail points in this variety	15
Form	Narrow, long, neck long and thin, all to be graceful in line; shoulders narrow, well-sloped; fore-legs medium length and thin; hind legs long in proportion and stouter built; feet round and small	15
Tail	To have no tail whatever, not even a stump, but some true bred have a very short, thin, twisted tail, that cannot be straightened, this allowable, and is true bred; but thick stumps, knobs or short, thick tails *disqualify*	25
Size and condition	Large, elegant in all its movements, hair smooth, clean, bright, full of lustre, and lying close to the body, all betokening good health and strength	15
TOTAL		100

The History

'Midnight concert' postcard showing some of Louis Wain's anthropomorphised Manx cats. Kindly loaned by P.B. Tucker

experimental farm and agricultural breeding station at Knockaloe just outside Peel so, in November 1961, cat breeding was added to the farm's responsibility.

What the government didn't expect was the amount of international interest. Requests for kittens came flooding in and, at first, had to be refused as the idea had been to build up and repopulate the breed. The government had also not expected the numbers of tourists who wanted to visit the cattery; Knockaloe is fairly remote from most tourist attractions, particularly if, as was the case in the early '60s, most people relied on public transport to get about. If tourists couldn't get to the cats, the cats would be brought to the tourists and, in July 1964, the cattery was moved to specially-built premises in Noble's Park, Douglas. For nearly thirty years the cattery ensured that the island had a continuing and plentiful supply of Manx cats. Only a combination of spiralling costs and concerns about the cats' welfare caused the cattery to close on 28 February 1992. Its remaining occupants were rehomed on the island which gave them their name.

Although the government breeding programme no longer exists, the Isle of Man still has a charitable cat sanctuary. Mann Cat can be found on Main Road, Santon. One of its residents is pictured here Photograph © P.B. Tucker

PART II

THE MANX CAT TODAY

Today there are probably more Manx cats in North America than there are in the British Isles and almost certainly more than there are on the Isle of Man. Because the cats are popular across the Atlantic, most registered breeders, i.e. those who breed the cat with the intention of showing the offspring, are in North America. The two centres of Manx cat population – North America and Europe – have resulted in slight differences in the two variations of the breed and also in the breed standards for showing.

The first thing to be said about the Manx cat is that it is a variation of a short-haired, long-tailed cat. At the risk of upsetting Manx breeders, strictly speaking the Manx cat is not a true breed in the biological sense. To a scientist something which breeds true is an organism which has certain biological traits which, when bred with another organism showing the same biological traits, produces only offspring with those traits. Manx cats don't do that. The Manx cat's taillessness is caused by a genetic mutation and female Manx cats can produce kittens which have no tail, a short tail or a long tail. In addition, the amount of tail shown by kittens within the same litter can also vary,

BREED STANDARD IN EUROPE

Breed standard for the Manx/Cymric cat as specified by the Fédération Internationale Féline (FIFe); the European standard. Compare it with the standard for North America on page 14 and the standard preferred in the 1880s on page 11.

Feature	Characteristics	Points
Head	Fairly large and round, a chubby appearance, prominent cheeks, medium long nose without a definite break or stop and not retroussé. Ears to be set fairly high on the head, medium in size, open at the base and tapering slightly to a point	15
Eyes	Large and round. Should correspond to the colour in British varieties, but is not very important	5
Coat	Manx; short, double coat of good texture. Undercoat soft and thick to make a well-padded coat Cymric; medium length, double coat. Undercoat soft and thick with soft silky feel, yet full, well padded all over the body	15
Body	All colour varieties and patterns are permitted, including all colour varieties with white; any amount of white is permissible.	25
Back	Solid and compact with a broad chest. Legs well muscled; front legs short and set well apart to show off the broad chest. Hind legs are higher than the front legs forming an angle from the back to the front of the body. Round paws.	10
	Compact and short but in balance to the body, ending in a definite broad and round rump. Flanks of great depth.	
Tail	Rumpy; an absolute absence of tail with a definite hollow at the end of the spine. Rumpy Riser; a rise of sacral bone (no caudal bone) which should not spoil the tailless appearance of the cat. Stumpy; a short, sometimes irregularly formed, stubby tail no longer than 3cm, which may not be bent or kinked.	25
Condition		5
TOTAL		100

BREED STANDARD IN NORTH AMERICA

Breed standard for the Manx shorthair and longhair as specified by the Cat Fanciers' Association Inc (CFA); the North American standard. Compare it with the standard for Europe on page 13 and the standard preferred in the 1880s on page 11.

Feature	Characteristics	Points
Head and Ears	Very round and jowly with prominent cheeks, more so in the male than in the female. Medium in length and with a gentle dip from forehead to nose. The muzzle is slightly longer than it is broad with a strong chin and a sweet expression. There is a definite whisker break with large round whisker pads. The neck should be short and thick. The ears are medium in size in proportion to the head, widely spaced, and tapering to a rounded tip. When viewed from behind the ear set resembles a rocker on a cradle. The ears on a shorthair have sparse furnishings on them with full furnishings for longhair Manx.	25
Eyes	Large, round and full. The ideal eye color conforms to coat requirements. Eyes are at a slight angle towards the nose with outer corners slightly higher than inner corners.	5
Body	Solidly muscled, compact and well balanced with sturdy bone structure. Stout in appearance with a broad chest. Medium in size with well-sprung ribs and a broad chest. The cat should give an appearance of substance and power without being coarse. The back should be short in proportion to the rest of the cat, and should form a smooth continuous arch from shoulders to rump, curving down at the rump to form the desirable round look. The rump should be extremely broad and round, like an orange or grapefruit. The height of the hindquarters should be equal to the length of the body. Males may be slightly larger than females and the longer coat of the longhair Manx may make the cat's body appear longer. The Manx should have great depth of flank – more than any other breed – causing considerable depth to the body when viewed from the side.	25
Legs and Feet	Heavily boned and straight. Forelegs are short and set apart to emphasise the broad, deep chest. Hindlegs are heavy with muscular thighs, much longer than the forelegs which causes the rump to be higher than the shoulders. Paws are neat and round with five toes in front, four behind.	15
Tail	Complete taillessness is preferred to emphasise the roundness of the rump. A rise at the end of the spine is allowable providing it doesn't stop the judges hand.	5
Coat	Double coat; the undercoat is close and cottony and covered by a longer, open outer coat. Together they have a well-padded quality, which should help accentuate the round appearance.	20
Color and markings	Shorthair; texture of outer guard hairs is somewhat hard, appearance glossy. Longhair; soft, silky and of medium length, dense and gradually lengthening from the shoulders to the rump. Breeches, abdomen and neck-ruff should be longer than the coat on the main body. Toe tufts and ear tufts desirable. Half the points are for length, half for texture. Color/patterns showing evidence of hybridization (chocolate, lavender, ticked tabby, pointed or these combinations with white are not permitted.	5
TOTAL		100

Scadoo, Manx for 'shadow'
Photograph © P.B. Tucker

while the mutation which causes taillessness is not consistent so it can skip a generation. In other words, a tailless Manx cat can produce tailed kittens, the offspring of which can again be tailless. It's owing to the reason they are Manx in the first place, that Manx cats can't be guaranteed to breed true. It's all down to genes.

The genetic mutation which causes taillessness is actually causing a spinal deformity. The tail in non-Manx long-tailed cats is usually made up of just over twenty vertebrae. In Manx cats these vertebrae are missing or fused. Because the mutation affects the skeleton, 'Manxness' is not confined to the lack of a tail, but affects the whole spinal column. Manx cats tend to have fewer vertebrae in their backs than non-Manx cats, individual vertebrae may be shorter than average, particularly at the front end of the cat, while those at the rear end may be fused, which in turn can lead to some loss of suppleness. In addition there may be some fusing of the bones of the sacrum. The sacrum is a bone which is shaped like an arrowhead, and which fits like a wedge between the two hip bones at the base of the spine and effectively joins the spine to the tail. Such fusing of the sacral bones occurs naturally in human beings when they are between the ages of fifteen to twenty five, but does not usually happen in non-Manx cats at all.

It is generally accepted that there are four categories of Manx cat:

Rumpy

Has no tail at all. Dimple Rumpies are so emphatic about their lack of tail that they have a small hollow where the tail would begin. Such cats have no tailbones.

Riser, or Rumpy Riser

Has a hint of a tail made up of a few vertebrae under the fur on the cat's bottom. Where a tailed cat would raise its tail, the ghost of a tail rises with Rumpy Risers. Just how much movement there is and can be depends on the cat's mood and the amount of tail it (doesn't) have. The few vertebrae it has tend

Not perhaps very elegant, but it emphasises Troubs' complete lack of tail
Photograph © P.B. Tucker

to be fused together so, although the cat can lift its rudimentary tail, it can't move it from side to side.

Stumpy

A self evident name for cats which have a short tail made up of fewer vertebrae than would be standard for a non-Manx cat. The tail is movable to a certain extent, including from side to side, but tends to be stiff.

Longy, or Tailed

The tail appears very similar to those of non-Manx long-tailed breeds and is mobile and flexible.

Stumpies can have tails of any length from almost nothing, to almost the full length. The easiest way to distinguish a stumpy from a rumpy is that the skin and fur is formed around the short tail, rather than the tail lifting beneath the fur of the rump. Stumpies can be prone to getting arthritis in the tail and some American breeders remove stumpy tails to prevent the possibility of the cat experiencing pain later in life. UK breeders are not allowed routinely to remove the tails of kittens, as tail docking without immediate medical cause has been illegal within the UK since 2007. The law refers principally to the tails of dogs, although other animals, including sheep and pigs are also mentioned. The docking ban is total in Scotland and almost so in England and Wales where certain named breeds are excepted if the particular dog is being docked for working purposes and is not more than five days old. Although cats are not specified in the Animal Welfare Act 2006 which introduced the ban, docking is only permitted to be carried out by qualified veterinary surgeons. Vets are usually reluctant to remove the tails of otherwise healthy animals and particularly reluctant to leave themselves open to questions of legality and professionalism. The Isle of Man passes its own laws, so UK laws do not apply, but as, at the time of writing, there were no registered breeders of Manx cats on the island (although plenty of pet owners who breed their cats occasionally), Manx law is not invoked. The law still of course applies to those with pet Manx cats who produce kittens, but tail docking is far less common among pet owners than professional breeders.

Taillessness is the most obvious difference between a Manx breeds, but it is not the only difference. Because taillessness the cat's hind legs are also affected. In a Manx cat the hind the front legs, so, when the cat is standing, the spine arches the base of where the tail would be; the back of a tailed flat. It is occasionally said that the Manx cat is a series of rounded, the head is round, the eyes are round, even the paws chest is broad and the flank deep, creating a soft contour and a back legs make the Manx cat an exceptionally good jumper, manoeuvrable, which probably contributes to their prized skill as cat and other short-haired is a skeletal deformity, legs are longer than from the shoulder to cat would usually be circles. The back is are round, while the stocky animal. Its long very fast and extremely excellent mousers.

Sometimes the combination of genes produces a severe genetic mutation of the spine which gives rise to a form of Spina Bifida. Spina Bifida is not a specific disease or complaint, but a general term used to describe any condition which causes the spinal cord to be incomplete and thereby not completely cover and protect the nerves contained within it. The term can also be used in cases where the vertebrae do not adequately protect the spinal column; if any gaps are large enough, part of the spinal cord may protrude between the vertebrae or be caught in them.

Problems with the spinal cord can also affect the way the cat moves. It is not so much that the cat experiences any obstruction to the full working of its back legs, but that it lacks some of the nerves at the base of the spine which transmit instructions from the brain. The messages can become slightly scrambled and the effect of this is most noticeable in leg movement. It used to be quite common, for example, for a Manx cat to appear unable to move its rear legs independently. In these cases cats have a hopping or jumping gait where the cat uses its back legs rather as a rabbit or kangaroo does. Even Manx cats which walked normally were likely to hop when travelling at speed. The hopping gait was at one time thought desirable and was actively bred in show cats, but the practice has long been discontinued by reputable breeders, when they realised that the hopping was symptomatic of more serious health concerns for their cats.

Another effect of the mutation of the spinal cord can be that, when they walk, some Manx cats put more of their back legs on the ground than is normal and, instead of walking on their paws, they use part or all of

The Manx Cat today

the surface of the leg below the hock. A 'plantigrade stance', as it is called, was always less common than the hopping gait and, although still possible, good breeding practices mean that it is rarely seen nowadays.

In more extreme cases of genetic mutation the spinal deformity can extend to the pelvis which means that Manx cats can have trouble controlling their bladder and bowels. Surgery is occasionally required to prevent or correct chronic constipation or leakage, while kittens often take longer to house train. A very few kittens cannot be house trained as they simply lack the means to control their ability to relieve themselves. In very extreme cases the cat's pelvis may be twisted, its spinal cord damaged or completely unprotected, and its digestion impared.

THE GENETICS OF MANXNESS

Chromosomes carry DNA material in the nucleus of each cell. A gene is material on a chromosome that provides a code for different traits. Thus eye colour, fur patterning, etc., are all dictated by genes. The norm for each animal, including human beings, is to have two copies of each gene, which is why genes are often written as a pair of letters (**TT**, **Tt** or **tt**). As most of us know, genes are inherited. Each parent provides one half of the genetic information (**T** or **t**). The effect of mixing the genes from both parents depends on what sort of genes they are.

Alleles can be thought of as genes with a specialised code. For example, a gene specifies eye colour, while an allele specifies a particular eye colour. In cats a gene specifies tail, while an allele specifies the length of the tail. Alleles can change spontaneously by what is called mutation. If the change is useful, or at least not immediately harmful, then the allele may be passed on to subsequent generations. In Manx cats, the allele which determines the length of the tail has changed to allow the tail length to be nil, i.e. no tail.

Some alleles are dominant over others, which is why the pairs of letters describing genes/alleles can appear in upper or lower case or a mix of the two. In the example above **T** is the dominant or stronger gene, **t** the recessive or weaker gene.

A genotype is the actual set of alleles an organism (e.g. a cat, human being, tree, etc.) carries; genotypes therefore specify what any individual example of an organism will look like. For any particular trait an organism is said to be heterozygous if it carries two different alleles, for example **Tt**, and homozygous if both the alleles it carries are the same, for example **tt** or **TT**. A genotype is said to be homozygous dominant if it carries two dominant alleles (**TT**) and homozygous recessive if it carries two recessive alleles (**tt**).

Taillessness in Manx cats was caused by a genetic mutation around three hundred years ago. Cats with standard tails can be described genetically as **tt**. The changes to the skeleton which result in taillessness are carried in dominant alleles which can be labelled **T**. It is widely thought that the homozygous combination **TT** causes serious health problems and is usually fatal. Cats with both dominant alleles (**TT**), therefore, usually die before or shortly after birth or, in rare cases of survival, have such serious internal and spinal problems that it is kinder to put them down. For this reason the dominant gene (**T**) is sometimes described as a lethal gene.

Manx cats therefore are almost invariably heterozygous (**Tt**), i.e. they carry one allele which specifies a short tail or no tail, and one allele which specifies a standard tail. For this reason it is impossible to predict the appearance of different kittens in the same litter. Two Manx cats, both **Tt**, could produce kittens with the genotype **tt** (standard tails), **Tt** (shortened tails or none), or **TT** (severe health problems and usually fatal).

An additional complication makes predictions of taillessness even more difficult. Some research has indicated that the dominant allele for taillessness (**T**) is more likely to pass through the tom rather than the queen. It is estimated that approximately 30% of female Manx cats, and 70% of male Manx cats will pass the dominant allele (**T**) to their offspring. As males are also particularly liable to carry the tailless allele, they are therefore also more likely to be homozygous dominant (**TT**), and therefore less likely to survive. Consequently there are likely to be fewer male Manx cats than female ones.

Left, ffinlo playing. Look at his paws! The close-up, above, is from another polydactylic cat, Briege
Photograph © P.B. Tucker

Manxness is sometimes called a 'lethal gene' (see box for genetic details) as certain combinations will kill the cat. Kitten embryos carrying the lethal combination of genes are often reabsorbed during pregnancy or, on the rare occasions they develop fully, can be still born or die shortly after birth. About a quarter of Manx kittens are affected in this way, which means that litters from Manx cats tend to be about 25% smaller than litters from most other breeds. As Manx toms are particularly liable to carry the gene for taillessness, and as certain combinations of that gene are lethal, male rumpies are uncommon.

For all these reasons reputable breeders take great care in their breeding programmes in order to avoid the risk of perpetuating health problems and serious spinal deformities. Many breeders have been successful in their work to minimise the health risks to the breeding population of Manx cats. As a result of such care the Manx cat population today is much healthier and more stable than has sometimes been the case.

Manx cats mature slowly and some health problems are late displaying themselves. To ensure that kittens are healthy, breeders now rarely release them to their new homes before they are four months old, and sometimes even older. Although all this talk of genetic mutation sounds alarming, once Manx cats have passed the age of six months without showing any warning signs of underlying concerns, they can be considered largely free of any serious problems caused by their genes. Adult Manx cats are just as healthy as their long-tailed cousins.

One genetic mutation which is fairly common in all cats, but particularly prevalent in certain breeds, including the Manx, is polydactyly. This is a naturally occurring genetic change which results in some cats having more toes than is standard. Cats usually have eighteen toes, five on each front

Millie, from millys, *the Manx for 'sweet'. You can tell from the shape of her body and face that she's Manx although she's sitting on the (lack of) evidence! Photograph © P.B. Tucker*

> **MANX WORDS**
>
> The Manx for cat is *kayt*, plural *kiyt*.
>
> Rumpy – *stubbin*
> Stumpy – *bwonnagh*
> Long-tailed – *fammanagh*
>
> Manx cat – *kayt* or *kiyt Vanninagh*, or sometimes *kayt chuttagh* (cat with a bob of hair).
>
> At sea Manx cats are called *screeberey* or *screeberagh* (scratchers).
>
> To call a cat in Manx, shout *daunee, daunee.* ('Here, kitty, kitty'!)

paw and four on each back paw. Polydactyl cats have more than this. The condition is very rarely a problem and many cats with extra toes often learn to manipulate objects with more delicacy than their less well-endowed peers. As the genetic mutation which causes polydactyly can occur in various different forms it may or may not be passed on to offspring.

The colour of eyes and fur is also defined by genes not related to the tailless gene but often appearing with it, so certain colours are more prevalent in Manx cats than others. Traditionally Manx cats are tabbies, often with no white markings, but Manx cats are known in virtually all the more usual colours. Some breeders have also introduced different non-Manx bloodlines to expand the range of colours available in Manx cats. Single colours are usually referred to as self or solid, hence self black or solid black is a black cat. Self white or blue (grey) Manx cats are rare. Some colours, such as black or red (orange) are carried only by the female chromosome, which means that male cats of those colours will have inherited the colour from their mother and will not pass it on to their own offspring. A mix of such colours, e.g., the mix of black and red which makes up tortoiseshell will almost always mean that tortoiseshell cats are female.

Eye colour is genetically related to coat colour so, for example, predominantly white cats can have blue eyes and sometimes have eyes of different colours such as one blue and one green or yellow (see opposite); cats lacking white in the fur cannot have blue eyes. Manx cats tend to have green, yellow or gold eyes, although other colours are known.

Manx cats usually have a double layer of fur with a thick short undercoat, sometimes shed in hot weather, covered by a longer coarser outer layer. They are typically short-haired, but long-haired Manx cats certainly exist and some

> **TRANSMOGRIFICATION**
>
> Awkward and ungainly, plain, dull, fat and old,
> Unlovely and unlovable, feeling rather cold,
> Contemplating sadly my little heap of cares,
> Dreary and disgruntled, I sat down on the stairs.
>
> A picture of despondency, I sought in vain for calm,
> Until I sensed a gentle presence pressing at my arm.
>
> In mature sophistication, a paragon of taste,
> With culture, style, refinement, urbanity and grace,
> Enviable, elegant, upon the stairs I sat,
> The comforted companion of a cat.
>
> *Frances Chambers*

breeders, particularly in the US, concentrate on breeding them. They have tended to be known as Cymric cats, although the US Cat Fanciers' Association now use the term 'longhair'. *Cymric* is Welsh for Welsh – the Manx for Welsh as an adjective is *Bretnagh* (as opposed to *Bretnish* which is the Manx word for the Welsh language) – but such cats have little connexion with Wales and are a variety of Manx. Longhaired Manx cats were once frowned on and not thought acceptable for showing. Mr H.C. Brooke, a famous nineteenth century cat breeder and exhibitor was quoted by Miss Frances Simpson in *The Book of the Cat* as saying: 'Now and then we see long-haired Manx advertised, but these are, of course, mongrels or abortions, and by no means Manx cats.'

One saying often quoted is that what Manx cats lack in tail they make up for in personality. They seem to pack an awful lot of cat into a relatively small area! They are intelligent, very fond of human company, good with children and often show characteristics which tend to be thought of as dog-like. They will retrieve small thrown objects for example, are fond of water and good swimmers. They follow their humans about and like accompanying them on walks; they can even be trained to walk on a lead. They can 'speak' but the voice of a Manx cat is very quiet for its size. They seem to prefer using either a low growl-like sound, or a high trill which they use to reply to or call their people. Most people, having owned a Manx cat, prefer it to any other breed.

Odd-eyed longhair Manx Supreme Grand Champion Alter, Branbarrel One Mint Julep. Owned by Kay DeVilbiss, Minus DeTails, Texas. Photograph © Helmi Flick Cat Photography

The Manx Cat today

PART III

FOLKLORE

Possibly the most bizarre folktale about the origin of the Manx cat was that it was a cross between a cat and a rabbit. The tale seems to have originated with Joseph Train of Castle Douglas, Galloway in his book *An Historical and Statistical Account of the Isle of Man*, published in 1845. He says: 'My observations on the structure and habits of the specimen [of Manx cat] in my possession, leave little doubt on my mind of its being a mule, or cross between the female cat and the buck rabbit.' After going on to describe his tailless cat Mr Train continues: 'although I have made many inquiries, I have not been able to establish a single instance in which a female rumpy was known to produce young. My opinion, as to the origin of the rumpy, has been strengthened by a coincident circumstance connected with this district. A few years ago, John Cunningham, Esq. of

When Noah built his famous ark
To ride upon the deep,
One fine-built Tabby did he mark
That special breed to keep.

But as poor Tom went in, out rang
A shrill blood-curdling wail –
On his hind part the door did bang,
And lopped off Tommy's tail!

As Noah threw the casement wide
At Mona's Isle to peep,
Our Tom to seek his missing pride
Over the sill did leap.

Full spry was he nor did he fail
To reach fair Mona's shore,
But vainly sought his long-lost tail;
He never found it more.

And his descendants to this day,
Buck-jump in rabbit style,
Yet, like their fellows, have their say
At midnight on the tiles.

And now, you doubting folk, impale
Your doubts upon this peg –
Mona, in lieu of Tommy's tail
Received an extra leg!

Reproduced from a Norris Meyer Press postcard from 1906-8, courtesy of *Tails of the Tailless* by Robert Kelly

Feline resident of Cronk Vinorca, Laxey, Isle of Man. Photograph © George Hobbs

A De-tailed Account of Manx Cats

TALE OF THE CAT

Not many now know of those days long ago
When the Manx cat appeared on the scene...
Tho' wearing a fur and producing a purr,
He'd no tail where a tail should have been.
Not even a stump at the end of his rump
With nothing to cover his blushes;
Long hind legs were bent as if they were meant
To hop over ditches and bushes.

There are some who will say nature formed him that way
When a Pussy made love to a Bunny
And that ever since then it's been plain to all men
That the Manx cat looks odd – even funny.
Be that as it may, let's honestly say
The story is falsehood and fable;
So wipe off the smile and let's ponder awhile
On the down-to-earth truth, while we're able.

At the time of The Flood The Ark stuck in the mud
On the slopes of the Mount Ararat;
And out of it came every beast one can name,
Including the dog and the cat.
But those two are foes as everyone knows;
And so it's to little avail
To pretend that the dog was just playing leap-frog
When he bit off the pussycat's tail.

With a howl and a leap puss plunged in the deep
And swam without purpose or plan,
Until on the mend but without his tail-end
He arrived on the green Isle of Man;
And there to this day he progeny stay –
But whether they're female or male,
Each one of them ranks as a cat that is Manx
With a rump but no trace of a tail.

T.J. Corcoran

Hensol, in the stewartry of Kirkcudbright, stocked a piece of waste land on his estate with rabbits, which multiplied rapidly. In the immediate neighbourhood of this warren rumpy cats are now plentiful, although previously altogether unknown in the locality. Not a doubt seems to exist as to the nature of their origin… At the same time I am far from wishing my statements to be understood as settling the question.'

The myth probably arose because the tails of stumpies (see page 16) can look a little like rabbits' tails, while the cat's hopping gait – caused by the pelvic deformity and more frequently seen in the past – is reminiscent of bunny hops. Indeed, the cat has occasionally been called the Kangeroo Cat. Manx cats get on well with other animals including rabbits, but interbreeding between the two species is a genetic impossibility.

Some well-respected experts even claimed that amputating the tail of a female cat would increase the likelihood of her producing tailless kittens. St George Jackson Mivart, a biologist, contemporary of Charles Darwin, and, until his conversion to Catholicism, sympathiser with Darwin's theories, states in his book *The Cat*, published in 1881: 'a female cat had its tail so injured by the passage of a cart-wheel over it, that her master judged it best to have her tail cut off near the root. Since then she has had two litters of kittens, and in each litter one or more of the kittens had stumps of tails, while their brothers and sisters had tails of the usual length… It is of course possible that the mother had some trace of Manx blood in her, but it is not likely, and the occurrence of the phenomenon just after, and only after,

When Noah built his famous ark
To ride upon the deep,
On one fine cat he set his mark
That special breed to keep:

'For you see,' said he, to his family,
Before they all set sail,
'No bird or beast did I ever see
Adorned with such a tail.'

Now the cat had really a lovely tail
And, with wide and graceful sweep,
He would swing it round like a threshing-fail
When the flies disturbed his sleep.

But misfortune came, I'm loth to say,
A sad tale must be told,
And if you will due attention pay,
I'll now that tale unfold.

Now the birds and beasts of every kind
Came thronging to the Ark,
In order that none should be left behind
They must at once embark.
Our gallant Tom of course had a mate
(Of that you may be sure)
And said she, 'Now Tommy, don't let's be late,'
But Tommy said, '*Traa dy Liooar.*'

But Tom was cute, you may all go bail,
As any modern youth,
Quite keen on guarding himself and his tail
From the beak the claw and the tooth.
For his kindred folks were all on the list
In that first gigantic zoo;
The order was that none should be missed,
For of each there were only two.

And thus it chanced that Tom was the last
Of all that mighty throng
For had he gone in with the first that passed
I'd never writ this song;
As oft it is charged to cruel fate
By the tardy folks who fail,
Our Tom was the merest trifle late
And the door chopped off his tail!

Oh sad disaster that befell
Poor Tom in that awful bump,
The door had done its work right well
For it left him never a stump;

And ye good folks all, due warning take;
In a race never risk delay,
For he who elects to sail in the wake
Must surely the penalty pay.

Now the Ark went cruising far and wide
With all its rank and file,
Until one fine morning Noah spied
A lovely little Isle:
'It was surely here that the dove had stopped,'
He observed to his little crew.
It was Mona's Isle, and the window he dropped
Top obtain a clearer view.

Now Tom, just roused from a mournful trance,
Had also gained a peep,
And to seek for his tail there was his chance,
So he boldly out did leap
And deeply sank in the surging main
From the view of all that host
For they never saw him rise again,
So they gave him up for lost.

But Tom was spry, nor did he fail
To reach fair Mona's shore,
But vainly sought for his missing tail;
He never beheld it more.
Then he vowed that he nevermore would roam;
Here was his domicile.
Thenceforward he would make his home
This fair and lovely Isle.

Now Tom's mishaps his form deranged,
His hindpart took a hump,
And the loss of his appendage changed
His old-time trot for jump.
And his descendants to this day
Progress in rabbit style,
Yet like all cats they have their say
At midnight, on the tile.

Now this is how it came about
That the Manx cat has no tail,
Yet seems to get on quite well without
For he's always hearty and hale.
And ye doubting folk who won't believe
Dispel your doubts I beg,
For the lost tail Mona will never grieve
While she boasts of an extra leg.

Written by W.H. Gill and reproduced from *Tails of the Tailless* courtesy of Robert Kelly.

the accident and amputation, seems to indicate that in this perpetuation of an accidentally deformed condition, we have an example of the origination of a new variety.'

On the Isle of Man, once the cat had been established as a novelty for tourists, the tails of non-Manx cats were often cut off deliberately in the hope that their offspring would be born without tails. Certainly at the height of the nineteenth century tourist season, there would not have been enough Manx kittens to satisfy the demand for a living souvenir. Amputation of tails to create instant 'Manx' cats was prevalent among the poor, and the results were sold to the credulous.

In order to enhance the cat's mystique and possibly also to establish it as an older breed than it in fact is, stories also circulated of druids stepping on a cat's tail and thereby turning it into a poisonous snake. The stories seem to refer to the tails becoming snakes, but could mean the transformation of the entire cat. Cats' tails were rumoured to have been removed to prevent such metamorphosis. It must have worked as Mann, like its larger neighbour Ireland, is snake-free.

Bramble Photograph © P.B. Tucker

It was not only human beings who were supposed to remove the cats' tails. Some stories state that kittens' tails were used as good luck charms, or simply as decoration by Viking warriors. To save the lives of their offspring mother cats were supposed to bite off their kittens' tails and so frustrate the warriors' aims.

Taillessness was not considered to be a handicap either. It was suggested, during the nineteenth century, that the nervous force expended by most cats on their tails had reverted to the brain of the Manx and re-enforced its intelligence and activity.

One of the traditional stories of the origin of the island's breed of cat was that they were descended from a tailless cat coming ashore from a ship wrecked off the Manx coast at the time of the Spanish Armada. As a result, that part of the coast was called Spanish Head; it is on the south west tip of the island and is the second-most southerly part of the Manx mainland, after Dreswick Point on Langness. Unfortunately, not only is there no record of an Armadan ship being wrecked off the island, the fate of all the ships in the Armada is well documented. There is also no history of any tailless cats in

Spain. Some versions of the Armada story have the cat boarding the Armada ships from a port in Egypt, but, as the Armada fleet started from Lisbon in Portugal, this seems equally unlikely.

Another version of the shipwreck tale states only that the vessel was originally from Spain and discounts the Armada reference. The Spanish ship was supposed to have been a merchant vessel sailing from the Far East where the ancestors of today's Manx cat went on board. The legend could have arisen partly from a knowledge that some breeds of cat in East Asia also lack tails; the bobtail mutation is common throughout Asia, the most well-known example of which is the Japanese Bobtail (see page 7). The Manx people were famous sailors, and crew members returning to their home ports could well have spoken of having seen cats on the other side of the world which reminded them of those at home.

A similar but less well known tale is told by W.B. Clarke in the Short Communications section of *The Magazine of Natural History, Vol VII*, published in 1834. Writing on 18 December 1832, Rev. Clarke describes a holiday he took on the Isle of Man and says 'Mentioning the subject [of tailless cats] to a person at Balla Salla, near Castle Rushen, and not very far from the Calf, I was informed that a vessel from Prussia, or some port in the Baltic, was wrecked many years ago on the rocky shore between Castle Rushen and the Calf, and that, on her driving close in to the land, two or three cats without tails made their escape from the bowsprit, and were taken by the wreckers; and that these were the first of the kind ever seen in the island. I do not

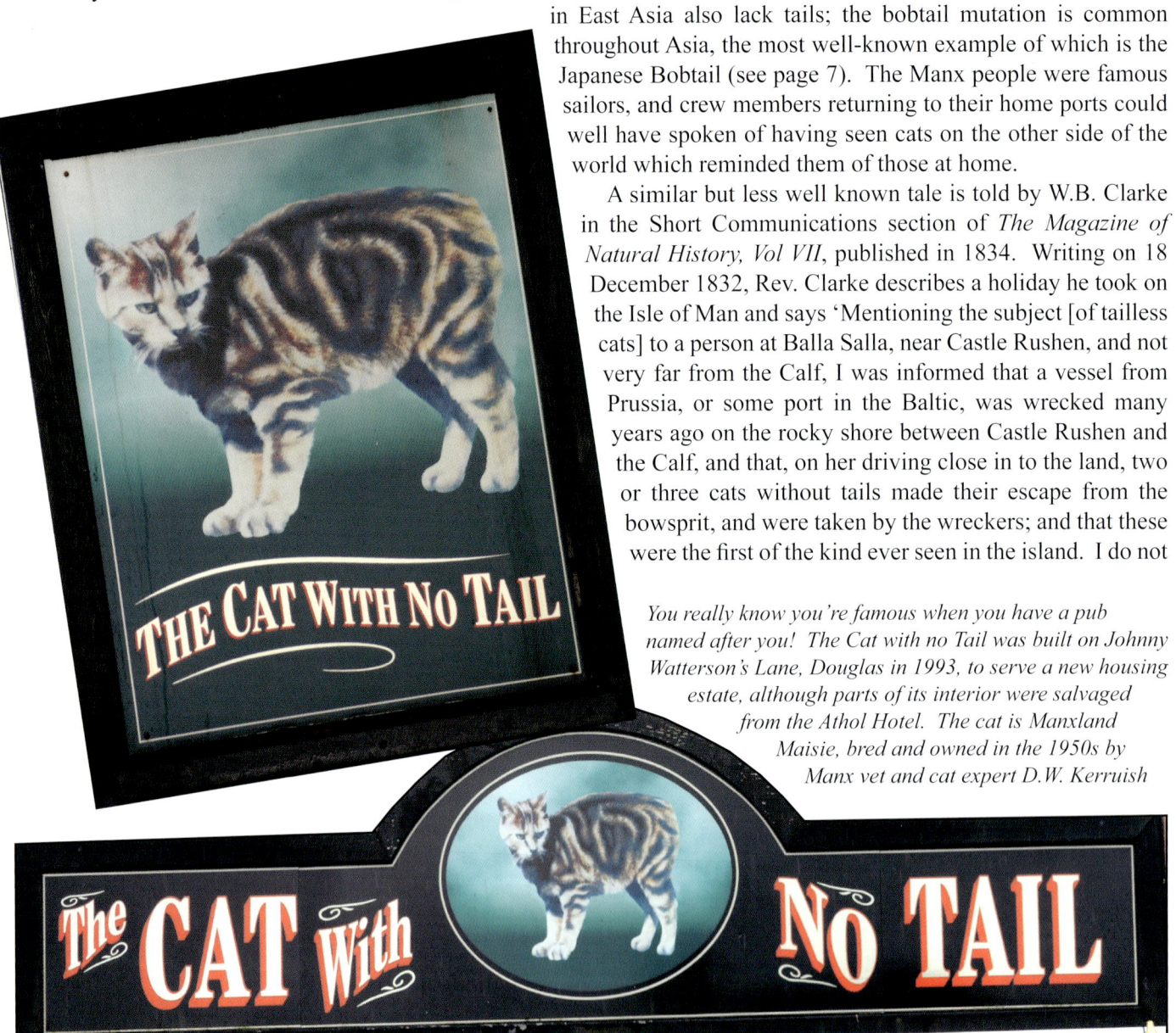

You really know you're famous when you have a pub named after you! The Cat with no Tail was built on Johnny Watterson's Lane, Douglas in 1993, to serve a new housing estate, although parts of its interior were salvaged from the Athol Hotel. The cat is Manxland Maisie, bred and owned in the 1950s by Manx vet and cat expert D.W. Kerruish

say that this is the truth, but I was told so; and, if it be the truth, the original breed is not of Manx extraction, but must be sought out in the north of Europe.'

The tabby is often considered to be the 'original' colour of Manx cats and Manx tradition states that there are three varieties of tabby. 'Spotted' tabbies have coats with a lot of black spots in the fur, 'blotched' tabbies have larger circular black markings, while 'mackerel' tabbies have stripes resembling fish bones! Manx tabby cats are also supposed to have a capital M in black between their eyes; the M of course stands for 'Manx'. Victorian cat lovers (and Victorian traders) obviously had vivid powers of invention!

Regardless of the colour or amount of tail, it was considered extremely ill-luck to meet a Manx cat on New Year's Day, particularly before meeting the *quaaltagh*. The *quaaltagh* – the word means 'someone who meets' – was the 'first footer', or first person to enter a house in the new year. Often the *quaaltagh* called just after midnight to ensure that no ill luck could befall the household before the good luck they brought with them.

Bracken - breck *as an adjective is the Manx for brindled - is the litter mate of* Bramble *on page 25. Photograph © P.B. Tucker*

Some Manx folklore states that Manx cats have their own king who assumes regal powers by night and turns into a cat of fire; some legends say that he rides in a carriage of fire. During the day the cat king lives the life of an ordinary cat, but, should any human be unkind to him, when the night comes so too does the cat king's revenge.

Most cats have a reputation for being fey and associating with the supernatural. Traditionally, Manx people dislike using the term 'fairies' as it's thought impolite and likely to bring bad luck, so usually refer to the little people as Themselves. Cats shut out for the night are usually considered to be on familiar terms with Themselves who reputedly let cats back into the house in return for a drink of their milk.

A particularly famous tale – if you'll pardon the pun – of how the Manx cat lost its tail concerns Noah. Life on the Isle of Man is

Folklore

Two more famous Manx cats, whose picture has been re-used many times. Below is Katzenjammer, owned by Mrs H.C. Brooke in 1903. Left is Queen Mab, also an Edwardian cat. She looks rather cross doesn't she?

traditionally rather laid back and leisurely and, like many people, the island cat refuses to be hurried. Consequently when Noah called the animals to escape the rising flood, the Manx cat thought all the rushing about unnecessary, or possibly beneath her dignity. Other animals scurried to the safety of the ark, but, *traa dy-liooar*, there was 'time enough' and the Manx cat strolled in their wake. With the flood lapping at her paws as she sauntered in, Noah closed the door sharply against the rising waters – and left her tail on the outside. A more modern version of the myth is that one of the motorbikes on the TT course sliced off the cat's tale as it sped past. Much less dignified!

Another Biblically-based story concerning the tailless cat involved Samson. Scorning the easy option of swimming the channel between England and France, Samson decided that swimming to the Isle of Man was a better challenge for his strength. Which of the surrounding countries was his starting point seems to have escaped the storyteller's notice. As Samson was approaching the island, tired from his swim, a cat playfully jumped onto his head and nearly drowned him with its weight. Not one to be defeated by a cat, Samson snatched the cat off his head by its tail. Unfortunately he forgot about his own great strength and squeezed too hard. Island cats have been tailless ever since.

Many famous writers have written stories about Manx cats – although Paul Gallico turned the animal into Manxmouse. Mark Twain's *A Cat-Tale*, for example, starts 'Once there was a noble big cat, whose Christian name was Catasauqua because she lived in that region. She did not have any

> Noah sailing on the sea stuck hard and fast on Ararat.
> His dog then made a grab and took the tail from off a pretty cat.
> Puss through the window then did fly and swam as only brave cats can,
> Nor never stopped 'til, high and dry, she landed on the Isle of Man.
> Then tailless puss earned Mona's thanks
> And ever after was called Manx.
>
> Reproduced from a Joseph Johnson booklet from 1882, reproduced from *Tails of the Tailless* courtesy of Robert Kelly.

surname, because she was a short-tailed cat – being a Manx – and did not need one. It is very just and becoming in a long-tailed cat to have a surname, but it would be very ostentatious, and even dishonourable, in a Manx.'

Manx cats extend an obvious fascination and writers often include them in their books. James Joyce even mentioned a Manx cat in *Ulysses*, although the reference is rather rude. Authors obviously feel that Manx cats add something special to their work. The Maeve Binchy short Christmas story *The Best Inn in Town,* for example, says: 'The three children liked…Granny Byrne's house because she had a Manx cat and a book about Manx cats which they would read six times a year with total fascination.' Admittedly it goes on to say that the other granny, Granny Dunne 'had a very strong line about cats spreading diseases and that if you had to have a cat, wasn't it perverse getting a poor dumb animal that was bred deformed and had its nether regions on display.' It doesn't take a genius to work out that the rival grannies didn't like each other!

In *The Voice in the Fog*, Harold MacGrath uses the cat to emphasise the theme of incompleteness when writing about Thomas Webb: 'Odd, isn't it, that an Englishman without his pipe is as incomplete as a Manx cat, which, as doubtless you know, has no tail. After all, does a Manx cat know that it is incomplete? Let me say, then, as incomplete as a small boy without pockets.'

Something lacking is also hinted at in Ethel Turner's *In the Mist of the Mountains* as four-year-old Max Lomax wants to play with his older siblings who are pretending to be reindeer. They have tails made out of tasselled curtain ties, but there weren't enough to go round. As the youngest, he was expected to go without: 'They had thought of them first, they insisted and, strongest reason of all, had got them first. Max had better be a sheep or a Manx cat and not bother about a tail.'

Many writers appear to think that the Manx cat's taillessness is unfortunate. In inviting the island's children to write their own version of how or why the Manx cat has no tail, we are celebrating the cat's most distinctive feature, rather than needlessly apologising for an imaginary lack. By doing so we're also continuing a long tradition of story-telling on the island – and off it too.

ffinlo. Photograph © P.B. Tucker

From April to July 2012, pupils in years 5 and 6 at Isle of Man schools were invited to write their own story about why the Manx cat has no tail. Stories had to be no longer than 500 words and were judged by David Ashworth of Lexicon Bookshop, Mary Cousins, Librarian in Charge at the Family Library, and Sara Goodwins of Loaghtan Books.

All three judges agreed that the following story by Megan Kneale, age 11, from St Mary's RC School, should be the winner:

Kayt Manninagh

Have you any idea why us Manx cats are without a tail? Well, let me tell you. If I had a fish for every time I was asked, I could fill the Irish Sea twice over. Mother always said:

'To be a Manx cat, Laxey,' (that's my name) 'is a very special thing indeed.' I suppose, when you think about it, as I often do, she, being the cat's mother, is right. No tail dragging when I want to run or jump, and, of course, no doors chopping it off. The list is endless.

There are many legends, like Noah closing the Ark doors too soon, a stomach-turning version of the Celtic Vikings cutting off our tails and using them for helmet plumes, and the story I enjoyed as a fluff-ball kitten, of a lady pussy-cat and gentleman hare who married. The dilemma of that tale (did you like that homophone?); who would the children take after? Luckily the Almighty came and decided that they should have the beauty of their mother and the strong back legs and tail of their father.

However, none of the above are true and let me tell you why.
                        They are legends.

Left, Scadoo and Troubs; below, ffinlo. Photograph © P.B. Tucker

The true reason we're tailless, or so I was led to believe, was the extraordinary battle of my great, great grandfather Kayt Manninagh and his arch-enemy Moddey Dhoo.

Long before we had the Internet there was a fearful conflict among the cats and dogs of the isle. It was decided between the two great warriors there would be a battle to end all battles and the winner would gain the key of freedom and so be able to do as they pleased and wander and rule among the humans of the Isle of Man.

A date and place of combat was agreed. The great warriors and their feline/canine comrades prepared for battle. The cats sharpened their claws and the dogs pointed their teeth. The day came. Mannanan, the ancient sea god, threw a mist coat over Peel Hill to conceal the view from human eyes and the warriors lined up for action.

Paws bashed, teeth chomped and heads rolled, but there was no clear winner. Kayt looked up from under his helmet to see the Moddey run towards Peel Castle. The dog was going to steal the key of freedom! My great, great grandfather was not going to settle for that, so he ran as fast as he could towards the castle and through the dark gloomy corridors.

CRASH

Moddey had been waiting and hit him full force with his shield. Moddey escaped into the cathedral, but my grandfather was too quick for him and slammed the big heavy door shut, locking Moddey Dhoo in Peel Castle FOREVER.

To this day Moddey Dhoo still roams there.

Ouch! Kayt felt an almighty pain. His tail! He hadn't been fast enough after all. A small price to pay for freedom.

And hence……….. the Manx Cat!

Megan Kneale

Folklore

SELECTED BIBLIOGRAPHY

A Cat-Tale, Mark Twain, P.I.C., 1987

Fairy Tales from the Isle of Man, Dora Broome, Norris Modern Press Ltd., 1980

Manninagh, No. 2, Mona Douglas (editor), November 1972

Manx Cats, R.F. and E.R. Sibthorpe, self published, undated

Manxmouse, Paul Gallico, Piccolo, 1968

Our Cats and All About Them, Harrison Weir, The Fanciers' Gazette, 1892

Tales of the Tailless, Robert Kelly, The Manx Experience, 1996

The Cat: an introduction to the study of backboned animals especially mammals, St George Jackson Mivart, John Murray, 1881

The Naturalist in the Isle of Man, Larch S. Garrad, David and Charles, 1972

The Magazine of Natural History, Vol VII, Various, Longman, Rees, Orme, Brown, Green and Longman, 1834

The Manx Cat, Marjan Swantek, T.F.H. Publications Inc., 1987

The Manx Cat, third edition, D.W. Kerruish, Nelson Press, 1964

The Manx Cat – A Collection of Historical Articles on the Origins and Characteristics of the Manx Cat, various, Read Books Ltd., 2011

This is Ellan Vannin, Mona Douglas, Times Press, undated

Turner's Golden Visions, Charles Lewis Hind, T.C. and E.C. Jack, 1910 reprinted from earlier undated work

Postscript

Can a Manx cat be 'cured' by re-tail therapy?